PINE SOOT TENDON BONE

Also by Radha Marcum

Bloodline

pine
soot
tendon
bone

Radha Marcum

WINNER OF THE 2023 WASHINGTON PRIZE
Andrea Carter Brown, Series Editor

THE WORD WORKS
WASHINGTON, D. C.

Pine Soot Tendon Bone © 2024 Radha Marcum

Reproduction of any part of this book in any form
or by any means, electronic or mechanical,
except when quoted in part for the
purpose of review, must be
with permission in writing
from the publisher.
Address inquiries
directly to:

THE WORD WORKS
P.O. Box 42164
Washington, D.C. 20015
editor@wordworksbooks.org

Author photograph: Doug Schnitzspahn
Cover design: Susan Pearce
Cover art: Watercolor image titled *Grief*,
rights purchased from iStock

ISBN: 978-1-944585-79-2
LCCN: 2024940041

Acknowledgments

Gratitude to the editors of publications in which these poems first appeared, sometimes in different forms:

Bennington Review: "Snow"
Flyway: "Physics Lesson: Valle Grande" and "In Case of Drought"
Humana Obscura: "Desire Path"
Lily Poetry Review: "Four a.m."
North American Review: "Ponderosas"
Notre Dame Review: "Lamentation in Wind"
Parks & Points: "Mountain Meadow"
Plant-Human Quarterly: "Meditation on Form" and "Another Fire"
Poetry Northwest: "The Distance Between Thought and Perception"
River Heron Review: "Cadenzas" and "Spring Rain"
Split Rock Review: "Hours of American Prairie"
Weber: The Contemporary West: "Fire Season in the West," "Poets," and "Poem"

Thanks

To Doug Schnitzspahn, my partner in all. To my children, Isa and Kieran, for their resilience and creativity under duress. To those who held space for this work: Rachel Walker, Buzzy Jackson, Michelle Theall, Hannah Nordhaus, Haven Iverson, Jeanne Yeasting, Bonnie Auslander, Susy Alkaitis, Deborah Kelly, Shenandoah Sowash, Nadia Colburn, Mary Barbara Moore, and Lise Goett and her marathoners. To

Ross Belot and Jacqueline Hughes Simon, symbiotic co-conspirators in poetry, for helping me see this book to completion. To Erin Elaine Robertson for companionship in birding and writing. To Cyrus Cassells and Amy Irvine for their support of this book, and for their poems and essays which exemplify how to write in unflinching witness, with tenderness. To Carol Moldaw, especially, for her impeccable poetics and guidance. To my editor, Andrea Carter Brown, for her precision, empathy, and appreciation of geologic and cosmic terminology. To Nancy White for wrangling with grace the many details of production, ushering this book into its final form, and to Susan Pearce for cover design. To Catherine and Jeremiah Osborne-Gowey for sharing fireside warmth in times of grief and celebration. To my parents and in-laws—to my father-in-law, "Lucky" Leon Schnitzspahn (1943–2024), particularly, for modeling the grit and generosity that constitute luck. To my Lighthouse Writers Workshop students and the Poet to Poet community for daring to keep poetry at the center.

Contents

Physics Lesson: Valle Grande	3
By the River	5
Hidden Narrative	7
Poets	8
Mountain Meadow	9
Saint Joan in the Fire	10
Hidden Narrative	13
Lichen	14
Fire Season in the West	16
On the Loss of Vacant Lots	17
In an Aftertime	19
In Case of Drought	20
Leaving the Party	22

Lamentation in Sandstone	25
The Distance Between Thought and Perception	26
Poem	27
Desire Path	28
Swarm	29
Ponderosas	31
Snow	32
Meditation on Form	33
Four a.m.	34
Lamentation in Rain	35

In a Plague Year	36
Wasps	37
After the Deaths of Two Children	38
The Velocity of Sorrow	39
Hidden Narrative	40
Lamentation in Wind	41

Cadenzas	45
Morning Field	48
Another Fire	49
Hidden Narratives	51
Hours of American Prairie	55
Blazing Stars	56
Preble's Meadow Jumping Mouse	57
Without Striving	59
Lights Out	60
A Bridge Is a Poem Between Earth and Sky	61
Spring Rain	63
Orogeny Origami	64
Sundown Updraft	67

Notes	69
About the Author	73
About The Word Works	74
Other Washington Prize Winners	75

O wind, rend open the heat.

–H.D.

Physics Lesson: Valle Grande

for D. W. M.

Space leans over the Valle:
the Valle slants: from the car,

dense cattle crawl like plusses
and minuses in grasses that sift

the scattered ashes of our physicist:
by the road, wind-scuttled fence-

wire abandons vigilance, slack:
for each experiment, he predicted

wind-risk, mixed thought
with atomic byproducts:

i.e. radioactive bits sprawled
in lakes, in lungs: tried to solve

for all fractions of contamination:
failed: fire made a ghost forest

here: the pines that swished
above his anxieties burnt to black

stick-arrows aim at ice clouds now:
he predicted these sparse spruces

drinking from their shadows,
i.e. pocked snow: predicted

climate shift: said so: grasped
the gravity of risk forcing

him off center, forcing us all off
center, at every curve in the road.

By the River

San Rafael Swell, Utah

handprints   (blood and resin)
fringe a cliff   by the river
mark   an era before
dry hunger   posit history
as the distance   between
cities   and these imprints
inimitable   opaque
—but one hunger   augers
another   —tatters of
food wrappers   catch
in rocks   as temperatures
dwindle   this river
that once swelled   ricegrass
in sand   —seeds layered
in polished pots   by hands
whose afterlife   wavers above
your head   —you want to press
a precarious pulse   to theirs
left palm   to left palm
each finger   to each
spread finger   but retract
as a spring gust   snags
plastic cups   and insects rise
in the tamarisks   —*distance is*
chimera you think   as sky shifts
the error   of atmosphere's

heat   —then a rasping
in juniper roots   —sand sans
cloud-burst—   an evaporative wind
flattens   the imagination

Hidden Narrative

Untitled: (Mesquite and Brush in Rolling Hills),
c. 1943, watercolor by Kakunen Tsuruoka, 1892-1977,
American citizen born in Japan

With ink swirled from ink stone
(pine, soot, tendon, bone)

and a big-cloud brush,
the artist frees flushed hills,

borderless clouds, a few
dark shrubs like spilled tea,

then, with a wolf-hair brush
(tip precise as the *t*

at the end of *internment*),
sets the skeletal mesquite twisting.

Poets

A low sun smudges darkness
under the piñons and junipers. Though the piñons
produced few nuts this year, the jays still pass
from clump to clump at dusk hunting the chestnut-black
teardrops. Tracing the dunes' dry embrace, you think
the hills resemble Modigliani's sketch of Akhmatova reclining.
The sunset teases and unsettles. Chamisa sways,
the downdraft's consort. Tomorrow, on instinct, the jays
will go on probing dry cones for seeds, like poets
recollecting words carried in full throats, then hidden—
Akhmatova's ellipses, her breath paused at line's end.
(The *inner emigré*, she burned every scrap of *Requiem*, burned
ink-marks cached in notebooks.) Whatever dark clusters
the birds bury now, next April they will fail
to find all of them, the slow-growing piñon forest
predicated on their forgetfulness.

Mountain Meadow

for Doug

Love's histories aren't mysterious.
In the Holocene meadow
slow carved by snow's retreat
kinnikinnik reddens at summer's end.
Tall grasses press in where elk rest.
Between shoulders of sun-flecked granite,
sky colors expand in last asters
and bee-throated gentians.
Moss colonies marry water and rock.
By the creek, two homesteaders—
clavicle and breastbone—rest under stones,
half clutched by a conifer lost to lightning.
Each night we lie down to disintegrate
in the meadow, our lives make shadow paths
like fallen firs sunk in grass,
bark peeled back to heartwood—
10,000 summers collapsed
and held in sapling roots.

Saint Joan in the Fire

> *If I were in a wood, I could easily hear the Voice which came to me. It seemed to me to come from lips I should reverence. This Voice has always guarded me well, and I have always understood it.*
> —Joan of Arc, Trial Testimony, 1431

> *France no longer has trees tall enough to make [Notre Dame Cathedral's] roof ["la forêt"] as it was.*
> —Bertrand de Feydeau, the vice-president of the preservation group Fondation du Patrimoine, *Insider* article, April 2019

What spark?
What misfired wire burns

in *la forêt*—in the Cathedral
that made of me a girl again

who believes voices in the trees?

•

The girl I was wore cathedral light
in flaxen hair,

heard air singing in the redwoods
whose seeds require

a germinating fire.

•

Martyrs: removed. Relics: removed.

Saint Joan shelters in an arch,
steadies the burning air—

gaze lifted
only halfway to Heaven.

•

Atmosphere ever hotter,
the pitch-covered centuries

burn down to the one
who believed her senses

and, offered clemency, refused it.

•

I have known the tallest trees
as fog-threaded ecstasies,

felt follicles rise
at their windy messages—

the premonitions.

•

Sunlight tears the sanctuary—

hushed with hiss
and smoke, cleansed with

holy Seine water,
littered with charred beams.

•

Mass held in debris—a dream.
I wake. I walk out of a grove

into a field where a white crane bobs
for insects—no, a white plastic bag

waves, in victory or surrender?

•

Wearing the dark syllables
of a forest transformed,

of a shelter no longer there,
St. Joan lifts her banner

into open air.

Hidden Narrative

Even the stars
give up some of their secrets
to the trees—

heavenly radiation
recorded in cedar rings—

blazing crucifixes seen
by 8th-century monks

now traced in carbon-14.

Lichen

       Papery blossom
in a rock sea—
          or is it the sea itself

       shrunk to a pool
on an ancient map?
          Today, the sky burns

       so we turn up-trail
toward boulders
          where lichen

       unfurls, slow-tells
the future of the
          before-us forest

       as it builds a self
from warming air.
          Over compressed

       rock layers, ancient
wave impressions,
          I see its form is

       a cyan prayer—
cells and breath
          interweaving,

we supplicating *we*—
brief as sea-foam
over red sandstone.

Fire Season in the West

A spotted towhee   grips the splintered fence
chest red as a controlled burn   then flits
into wildfire haze   —another blaze
peppers the membranes   of our eyes
blurs the yard   where I snip stubs   of done
marigolds and   blinking back   realize it's
ashes I've mistaken for flies   eye-floaters   it's
ashes of others' lives   falling   to my fore-
arms   to my restlessness   with garden scissors
—tonight   when the new wildfires   lay down
in me   each anxiety will flash   like dry
lightning   *how many acres this season?*   —crews
work to dig the break   the line   to tamp down
sparks   as stars wither   in the smolder
of every   engulfed   home   —though
certain groves   can burn   and survive
charred   like ponderosas   given time
I'll forgive the grasses   that replace the trees

On the Loss of Vacant Lots

First plundered, then
plowed, valleys divided
into rows for clone homes—
same body, same plumbing,
ironic names: *Dry Creek.*
Glacier Meadows. White Rock.
Who am I to despair
at the loss of vacant lots
yet prefer this: the jagged
timberline and lakes
of the Snowy Range,
where beetle-killed pines
lean away from wind
and into living trees?
Who am I to prefer
a lake surface that betrays
the wind's erratic shifts?
At 10,000 feet a reddish moon
rises dimmed but round,
trimmed by a bright rim of ice,
mirror of the lake's frozen sides
or how this cirque collects
and keeps a lip of snow
melted to a smooth edge
with just enough shade
to last the summer.
I curve in the curve

of glaciated gneiss, love even
the corkscrew hieroglyphic
scripts the beetles chew
in living cambium. Sheltered
by Browns Peak, I trace
Cygnus and Sagittarius,
and worry the fate
of glacier lilies.

In an Aftertime

Memory gnaws on me in the blue silence
of the withered hillsides where
cracked, earth-stained quartz stones—
mammoth molars?—trip me.
I think I may be just a trick the sky is playing,
a vacancy for the cicada's incessant trills
and pinecone bits snowing down
from the squirrels. Whatever falls through
the trees falls through my eyes.
It's September. Wild sunflower faces
tilt back as if just freed from
the dark earth into sharp daylight
like the subway riders who emerged that day
to see people fleeing and falling
in the fast-forward collapse of civilized steel.
For years the workers found teeth
in the rubble, no bigger than the pebbles
I scatter now by walking. Whatever debris
falls through the lines I'm writing
in my head, it is an inadequacy.

In Case of Drought

Call for spring. Conjure
winter's end. Bandage

limbs cracked or stunted
by wind or worry. Pray for

bees, for pollen bodies.
Pray the plum blossoms

become oval ovums ripening—
clusters green then red-green,

then fruits covered in dusk.
Do not doubt that doubt

will ripen in you. Pull indigo
lobes from limbs, bent.

Gather fruit in your shirt.
Snag windfalls in the grass,

split gladly for sparrow
and mouse. Observe

how doubts shine before
the knife. Sterilize jars.

Boil the fruits for jam.
Note the tiny toothmarks

made by ones who recognize
abundance when it is offered.

Leaving the Party

Warm ozones rouge up the refinery by the river
where the geese do not V into evening but veer or lag
or half-loop, disorderly—silhouettes departing dark
from a sparse backwater now lapped by red-gold haze.
Beyond the backlit city, the refinery's flame-hands
insist its intestinal metals churn for us, distilling crude
into gold—the fuels accelerating our sure departure.
The sunset is made more beautiful by that burning,
more perfect for the lenses we pull from pockets
and extend to compress dark wings into memory.
The geese veer in our pockets. The city surges.
It will be sleepless. It will steer our departure,
mesmerize our bare eyes with its refinements.
It reimagines everything but what hides the stars.

Lamentation in Sandstone

We had losses we could not locate   in the windy
alluvial wash   —snowmelt seeped   grains
from clefts   quartz   feldspar   lithic bits
loosed from late Triassic cliffs   —loss dogged us
over arroyos   in narrow canyons   carved from
the enduring habits of   old flow regimes   upper
and lower forces   conspiring   sediment into stone
stone into sediment   again   —it tracked us
past the boulder gaps   that collect   twig-and-leaf
histories of flash floods   —-scenting us   loss
doubled back   in the wash   then   scoured
by a steady wind   it lay down   in an alcove
and slept   —loss lost us   —one flow regime
gave way   to the next   and so the canyon
swept the dead coyote   right out into the wash

The Distance Between Thought and Perception

What was it from the bush—a bird or mammal?
The second half of its March call clattered
like a plastic ball dropped down concrete steps.
It was on the edge of the housing development
before the real thorn bushes and animal grass.
I wanted calm rock. I wanted to unlock thinking.
So when a few new blue utterly common flies
rose out of pine duff to unzip the back of silence,
I thought, *that's wrong, it's not silence* with tire hiss
and jets behind the mountain. The sunlight expanded
like a balloon in a blue artery. I thought of the house
halved and hoisted down the road by a truck,
and how at 4 a.m. it did not seem strange to see
a silvery buck peruse the church zinnias,
take note of us and, dashing into underbrush,
disappear as a stillness, a luminous flash.

Poem

The locoweed that kills horses blooms first
from a crack in one of your constructions.

Also known as *astragalus* it puts on purple,
rambles its dense leafstalks, throws silhouettes.

The bobcat stalks near. You've watched him
amble the low adobe wall, your glassed-in face

new to his house—his hills; his piñon and cholla;
his settled gravel; his substrata nailed with wells.

Wind repositions juniper cast-offs in sandy soil.
It would take a lot of locoweed to kill a horse,

you think; and native bees sip the purple bells.
Despite the wells' plummet, the cholla swells

yellow fruits from its tips—its angle on living
insisted on by rows and rows of sharp spines.

Desire Path

In mapping, they call it a *desire path*.
This morning we see it simpler, the illicit
trail bent into otherwise untracked grass
between this and that hunger (this and that
hideaway), divots gouged in the field's uniform
growth, crossed and crossed by animal pacing.
Is it harmful, our *samsara*? It doesn't seem much
but it adds up—our over and over bypass
of mud hole or thistle patch, the rivulet stream
that would make a mess of us in our madness
to get over it, to get some, to get there—
to cut straight to where we are simply more
desired—all of it *going* after all, in the end.

Swarm

Whatever can come to a city can come to this city.
—Muriel Rukeyser

A cold door opens in memory onto frozen peas, raspberries, corn, repeated ordinary forms waiting to be torn open

—someone *in tactical gear* enters your grocery store

enters all the small years you bought clumped fruits, broke them apart still in the bag, warmed them under the tap

—enters with an *assault weapon*, backdrop Easter baskets

from the same concrete that leads to your house where, at your desk, you retrace this morning's walk

—officers swarm the supermarket roof; sky cut by copter blades

on that walk, stopped by: also amazed by: the queen carpenter ant, thorax shining like a drip of candle wax, rose sepals, her wings drying

—inside, crumpled sacks; no, your cashiers

what it means is a new era, a new colony, the mate-swarm like too much punctuation in the cold, bright air

—neighbors in the maze to an exit beyond the dairy case

the ants will tunnel into a fallen ponderosa on the mesa, which means *table*—this neighborhood, *Table Mesa*, caught in a redundancy, a fact on repeat

—mind stutters *we are processing the crime scene*

in an ordinary place, a door opens; terror enters, then mazes into memory.

Boulder, Colorado, March 2021

Ponderosas

In grief I read the trees
wading in a sun-tide
on the mesa.

They tell me nothing
and I like it. They soak in
my deep-down

out-breaths and exchange
sugars made of light
under the earth.

Broken limbed
and ember-colored toward
the core, as warm

as clay in a dwindling
fire, they mother stillness
even as they shiver

and twitch needle sheen.
They sky write
with the retreating wind.

Snow

A woman lifts a limp curtain onto her winter-broken yard.
Cold fractals settle against the bare lilacs and fence gaps.

It is more blue, more scintillating than the linen-white snow
on a Sisley canvas she recalls most for its muted walls, a shadow

walking. So like an assumption, the snow deflects her gaze.
Lately, she has learned how local water managers see it—

each inch trickling into more cattle, more peaches. For whom?
One time, in temperate California, it snowed at her high school.

Sudden cold culled blossoms in the orchards as the wan flakes
vanished on the asphalt in an instant—more temporal than

the gauze wrapped around a classmate's neck, a bullet wound.
It happened first in that place, then it happened over and over again

in her mind. Here, like thought, the snow is so elliptical it is nearly
infinite. It drapes the flowers laced through a chain-link fence

at her supermarket where, last week, bullets perforated drywall
and people, flour stacks and people. She looks at her rose thicket,

at white-covered lumps of dog shit and thinks *I am tired—
tired of snow*. She thinks the light is looking for its respite, too.

Meditation on Form

According to space-time projections, all matter looks
vascular. Or is it lymphatic? I picture it as MRI magnets
beam back moon-bones from the darkness of my body
and pain propels me like Voyager I past the heliosphere.
In simulations, threaded galaxies—wispy as lace lichen—
stretch beyond our beyond. Superclusters stud the black
like bright-blooming algae on a tide-drenched rock. Toeing
the wet sand of childhood, I feared loneliness. Nights,
The Milky Way hovered in its terrifying, tattered silks.
I feared the dark but feared my starless interior more.
Now that this body can be turned inside out, I'll witness
its glitches, fractures in the gathered, vagrant atoms
that I am—elements that arrived on intergalactic winds,
the fusion that alone alliterates every pulse of lymph
and lichen spore, every bone-cell as new as the stars.
60 billion suns and no aliens detected, astronomers lament.
But whose body is this? What could be more alien than us?

Four a.m.

I am a kingdom overmastered by nests.
I am crows in a broken cottonwood.

In the aftermath of nothing-in-particular,
I seethe. I clench next year's leaves.

I'm certain I have incubated calamities
in a nest lined with ill foliage.

I peck desiccated flies; I gizzard
mortalities the dog sleeps through.

No sun hatches over the plains.
No relief molts the mountain's side.

I pray for snow glitz to shiver it all.
I claw the sheets.

No call roosters me back from this.
The neighbors' ducks sleep in their crates.

Lamentation in Rain

All night, memory pulses through soaked earth
like a worm, a segmented body with five hearts.
It has lived a cold and muscular life. It writhes
across hard distances toward you, a blind
finger on the contours of last year's violence:
a rifle in your store's aisles: shoppers collapsed
with force: the survivors: a perimeter of flowers.
Eyeless, unprotected, it has swallowed the dark
mulch of days and survived, a skin-breathing
tenderness. Now it traverses merciless spaces.
You lift it from the puddle with a stick, see
last year's tulips and sorrows digested, given back.

Boulder, Colorado, March 2022

In a Plague Year

> *The light of the North Star takes a long time to reach us, even though it's traveling 186,000 miles per second. The beams it shows us tonight first embarked when Shakespeare was alive on Earth.*
>
> —Rob Brezny, January 2021

I know the stars have no anchors, no intentions
to lose their burning hulls in our blurred oceans,
yet their particles enter our eye-ports torched.
Our eyes? Water, mostly. The faint blazes I perceive
now lap into me, at last, but embarked long ago.
By these glints, Shakespeare gauged tyrants and loves.
His North Star, like mine, brightened and dimmed
while seeming not to move, the steadfast axle
around which all other stars revolve—faultless
if you don't look too long. But no star is the same star.
See him there, blinking at the horizon to find
radial light launched captain-less into the void,
a burning ship that shines hard in the skull's dark
after his son has lifted anchor and drifted away.

Wasps

Drips from a god's soldering iron,
they appear fully formed in aimless

drift, middling between ceiling and floor
like worrying thoughts. They gather

at the cracks from the branched
nerves at the back of the mind.

Lifted into consciousness un-conjured,
peripheral, the congregations reconvene

to threaten me, waving a broom
as if to disperse them for good.

After the Deaths of Two Children

Breath hides in the spent garden
in the word *marigold* which eludes me
like a dropped note I try to re-pin—
to what?—to sun and pungent leaf ecstasy
to the dimmed bee-bent petals
but I cannot walk the garden's
syntax back to summer's exclamations
the silvery seeds drying in marigolds
mounded by the garden box.

The Velocity of Sorrow

My son runs to me through the school's field, electric with insects. He bends to the dog's kisses. And for a moment I am not a mind on stilts, not yet precariously stumbling to shield him from the news. Today, bullets entered nine students at a school near here. When the semi-automatic facts rushed in, loaded, I could not find a locking closet where they could not enter me. Paralyzed at my desk, I tried to re-enter words: *Dear Exit Wound*, I scribbled, *Where are the nearest exits? What is the velocity of sorrow?* There is no formula for this. I know the news satellites arc our sorrows across a blackboard shot through with stars. Ballistic data bits pierce us at the speed of light. So, even as my son and I stride out the chainlink gate, the gunman circles us. There is no solving for this: *What exists, exits as easily as this.* The unknowing dog senses home and pulls the leash hard. The crickets intensify their racket. *Whatever exists, exits.* My son adjusts his bag, weighted with facts, grabs my hand. *He could, just like that, exit existence.* Does he know?

Hidden Narrative

Today's headlines enter
uninvited, enter
and rearrange me

as ink focuses my eye.
I might as easily
read our future

in the desiccated hands
of cottonwood leaves,
in cupped milkweed husks.

Lamentation in Wind

for Gordon
with lines by Emily Dickinson

Cold wind doesn't stop me circling
this path between dried flax and asters,
among runners out in low-angled sun.
You aren't here. Only I'm seeing things—
echoes of your body before the bullets
spiraled in and tore our spring apart.
It's October again, I tell the rushing air.
You'll miss our Halloween party, although
it's been years since our kids were little.
Yesterday, I saw your son pressing
the crosswalk signal at the high school,
a leaf-shimmering light spilled all over him.
I couldn't stay to watch him safely cross.
It happens fast. The wind rips down
the light, leaves half-curled as hands.
Small ponds collect the scattered birds,
then darken like exit wounds. *What
indeed is Earth but a Nest*—a weaving
held in the crux of cottonwood limbs—
from whose rim we are all falling? But for
the erratic gusts in the gunman's brain,
you might still be running here beyond
our block, past the chokecherry thickets
where griefs hang viscous, burgundy-black,
with seeds the migrating birds swallow whole.

Cadenzas

I. Chickadees

Always the winter chickadees
in the hawthorn by the creek—

puffed as snow, ribboning
freezing air into cadenzas

through improbably small throats.
Cheeks brushed in concerto ink,

they sing harmonies
to complicate your discontent.

You are form in form—in form,
they contend.

You are the contented facts.
Not so, not so,

you shuffle, breath wordless
as air muffled under creek ice.

All winter, the irretrievable
low stone notes plunged

under—never reached an ear.
You listen for the un-selfed cadenza,

the melt out, winter's end notes,
the bird that can sing you to pieces.

II. Towhees

Cusp of March, of thaw and snow:
Rust-bellied towhees
inked in—wings not black
as kettles but coal
from the cold hills, limbs
the old wildfire razed—
now harbingers of leaves, melodies.

•

Contours, pixels: Mars Rover—
lenses un-sheathed—sends
star fire, new vistas.
Blue dunes, red planet—
a war god gone sad?
A towhee calls—*chit-chit
trill*—as the digital signal stalls.

•

Mind marches: Wars that started
moons ago muddle
my sleep—neurons burnt,
gone planetary.
Aim out, common bird.
Sing me horizons,
truces as true as your towhee song.

Morning Field

As the mountain's tilted hands
lift coyotes' *yip-yip* at the morning kill,

I hinge out to meet my edgeless-ness.
Mind a border state, I wade, elliptic,

obituaries and chickadees on repeat:
Who are we? are we—were you? were you?

Strung with crystalized wire, the road
waits for the sun's one order: *imbibe.*

In oblique evergreen shine, in ice glint
scattering from plank and stem, I see it:

each fascicle of dormant field, every
strand of deer muscle concentrated,

stilled. Each decent feeling. Each
translucency. Each seed cluster refusing

the bent field. In these months
of ready lessening—breath

made visible, then vanished—
the gaze goes wide, turns lucent.

Another Fire

Along fences, between
grasses, a churn of irrepressible stems
and leaves appears

bristled, silver,
flower-buds heavy as initiates' heads
bent in contemplation.

Walking, you pass their
ritual of replication: *from darkness, a body,*
from this fragment

of memory, re-
member yourself—a seed split
into sentience.

You know—anther and
filament, pistil and ovary—in each
papaveri a dark dome

forms, the *punctum saliens*—
throbbing dot of a primordial heart.
See? A single poppy

bursts before others,
one small fire in the green surge,
elemental petals

red as cloud-waves thrust
from a dying star, a pluralizing blaze
in the fertile field.

Hidden Narratives

I thought it was
a ghost girl screaming
keep looking.

•

Sappho's lyrics salvaged
from a mummified crocodile's mouth—
I take them in
over coffee:

*Someone, I tell you, will remember us,
even in another time.*

So her words enter this afterlife.

•

By the creek,
uncountable small birds converse,
obscured by fir needles,

but it's the drowned cliff swallow
my mind returns to—

her indelible
green-black body
limp in red silt.

•

Cold water flows over
mottled leaves

like clear glass
over grandmother's photo
in the paperweight on my desk.

Her face, the weight of brevity.

•

Mother of a daughter,
I listen for grandmother
but recall Sappho
in the creek's burbles:

*I have a small
daughter called
Cleis, who is*

*like a golden
flower.*

•

The creek's course
is a story curtailed by concrete.

Its truth would go
right through our houses—
and it did

during the thousand-year flood.

•

Once, I was a milk-pink blossom
grandmother leaned over

like a bloom
from a hillside of roses
she planted
and pruned,

she herself a rose
severed silently one night
by deer teeth.

•

It wasn't scavengers
or minerals in my blood
but a voice did say

be calm, insatiable one,
I will feed you.

•

Women—
the Greeks believed—
could not control
their boundaries.

And so?
Our voices might breach

this life,
the afterlife.

•

I keep listening
for the ghost girl.

Ruminating,
the creek echoes Sappho:
I want.

Hours of American Prairie

We took a walk   over the silicates   the luster
and much dullness that is   the incremental
breakdown of an inland sea-bed   of we
who script *cirrus   lenticular   waxing gibbous*
over the lake surface   its infinite metals
cut by buffleheads   and grebes   and wind
from one of many   directions   we received
the grebes' red stripe   itinerant signals
written into us   remainders of migration
over American prairie   many homes making
easy comfort in that dirt   in the birded
views where we   marked arrivals   wigeons
gadwalls   coots   every year fewer   rising
in eye-waters   every year   more *we* to braid
with birds   between dips   the grebes'
red stripe   struck the red receptors   of us
the hours of *ourness*   breaking down   in grass
where our minds could green   or nest next

Blazing Stars

In the field's morning council
bright plumes—dotted blazing stars—
reiterate their particularity
their purple exuberance in emphatic
blooms at the city's border
and in their inflorescence of tongues
minuscule seeds to be buried
in municipal syntax so late in this last
iteration of prairie blueprinted
for removal but I hear you I assure you I
hear your petaled mouths
your serifs of insignificance as signifiers as
a blazing testimony.

Preble's Meadow Jumping Mouse

Etymologically,
a dirge is a direction
that aims us

into a field
of endemic scurry,
toward a pebble-name

from *mus*, the humble
root of *muscle*
and *mouse*,

(its torpid body
curled in
winter's fibers).

Hidden among
the nails and two-by-fours
spoken here,

the Preble's is a dirge,
a little furred
hymn, an imperative

pushed up by
mechanical teeth
between the broken

syllables of wild rye
and asteraceae:
A ghost feel.

A feeble guest.
A gust felt breathing
us toward the torn field.

Without Striving

Today—did you see?—
lenticular ice-clouds

raced like greyhounds
over the peaks' surf-edge.

The moon, that lopsided
white pebble, tumbled

in its limits. What good
would it be to strive

in still air? The mountains
assembled a cold wind,

so the red-tailed hawk unfolded
its wings and, effortless,

soared over the ponderosas.

Lights Out

No burrowing owls or swift foxes hide
in the shadows of our home. I sense

their absences as I turn out the lights.
Too old for stories, my son—under a coverlet's

stitched, simplified beasts—conjures a still-life
called "Gone" on his phone. Vanished creatures

stare back at us from the varnished canvas.
Light glints on a curve-billed honeycreeper,

on the tips of South African bluebuck horns.
A Syrian ostrich egg glows, scribbled with notes.

My son says that ivory-billed woodpeckers
and bridled white-eyes will enter this frame.

I close my eyes, but the extinguished screen stays.
Darkness widens over the coverlet's elephants.

He wants to believe in species resurrection—
life spiraled up from the genetic code—a hope

pulled to his chin like the bedspread I smooth
over him, a boy memorizing our losses.

A Bridge Is a Poem Between Earth and Sky

Many makers are responsible for its structure,
for its concrete geometry

traversing air between ravine and cloud;
it shakes and hums with tread,

metal prone to freckled rust
and fretting corrosion:

from the hawk's perspective
it is just as useful as the igneous rocks

that distort passing wing-shadow;
the bridge won't save you

from the line of bright water
that threads the gorge

in a back heaven of the poet's eye;
it can hold the weight of 600,000

human hearts but not the average cloud
which weighs 1.1 million pounds;

it is a jumping point with call-boxes
wrens dart below,

though the heart weighs less than a pound
less than the lifted receiver.

Spring Rain

Waking parched, only the burrowers in us
        know how we endure the long dry-spells
                un-needful, nearly inanimate under the surface,
        like Great Basin spadefoot toads
absorbing atomized water—cached
        in desert sand God knows when—
                through skin in the dark. Now clouds
        drip soft rhythms on the porch. Do you
remember? One April, down a canyon
        in the transient pools we leapt over, spawning
                toads appeared. Water-mirrors in wind-eaten rock
        shimmered with cottonwood leaves, and yuccas
blossomed opulent above the toads' quickening.
        Rain threaded the rabbitbrush, the sego lily.
                Succulents' pores opened, briefly. Remember
        the drenched sheltering cliffs?
The rain signaling when?

Orogeny Origami

San Rafael Swell, Utah

1.
Make a horizon of the page

as if it were the light bare
striated shoulders of desert

under which fish-jaws gape
in sediment over which

purple wildflowers displace
Anthropocene air—

2.
—crease fence and freight train
mark distance make

lonelinesses in the whole—
break ancient lakebed coal

into angles of repose
for millennia

3.
—unfold and remake
a slope with globemallow

and primrose
pincushion and pronghorn

alert in the juxtaposition
of wind-twisted juniper

and coal plant
billowing white before

a dusk-purpled uplift
a floorboard-gray mountain

4.
—double fold
the jagged canyon line

and plunge-fold the red-black
sorrow-streaked cliffs

holding soft to air and talus
above the shimmer curve of water

that shapes the rock
that shapes the breath rushing

up for evening

5.
—tuck me into one star
swallowed by dusk

as if sky's fabric folded
a secret horizon in its sunset

Sundown Updraft

Grief stands in the ragged field,
a white horse draped in late sun, still
whole in its own skin. What grows
at fence-line, it nibbles. It ignores
my gaze, my eyes always late
to apprehend the sun already gone
eight minutes when I watch it slump
behind the mountain. The old horse
holds the field in place, the cottonwoods
shot through with red-winged blackbird
cries, a conclave of ravens scattering,
untethering my eyes from the field's
flanks toward an outworn work shirt
shrugged off, hung on the fencepost,
waving its arms to summon the sky.

Notes

The title *Pine Soot Tendon Bone* refers to the traditional ingredients of inkstone used in Sumi-e, a Japanese painting technique that originated in China. *Sumi-e: The Art of Japanese Brush Painting*, by Shingo Syoko (Chronicle Books, 2002).

Oh wind, rend open the heat (epigraph) is from "Heat," by H.D. (Hilda Doolittle). https://poets.org/poem/heat.

"Physics Lesson: Valle Grande," page 3, is for my late grandfather Donald W. Mueller, a physicist and meteorologist who worked at the Los Alamos National Laboratory.

"Hidden Narrative," page 7, refers to *Untitled (Mesquite and Brush in Rolling Hills)*, c. 1943, watercolor by Kakunen Tsuruoka, 1892-1977, American citizen born in Japan, accessed at https://www.denverartmuseum.org/en/object/2019.102.

"Hidden Narrative," page 13: Italics are from "Chronicles of the Rings: What Trees Tell Us," *New York Times*, April 30, 2019, accessed at https://www.nytimes.com/2019/04/30/science/tree-rings-climate.html.

"In an Aftertime," page 19, is for my father-in-law, Leon Schnitzspahn, who worked in the financial district of Manhattan. During his usual commute on September 11,

2001, he emerged from the subway to witness the second plane hit the World Trade Center.

"Swarm," page 29, and "Lamentation in Rain," page 35, are about the Table Mesa King Soopers mass shooting in Boulder, Colorado, March 21, 2021. Ten people were killed. The epigraph to "Swarm" is from "Waterlily Fire" by Muriel Rukeyser, accessed at https://www.poetryfoundation.org/poems/54593/waterlily-fire.

"Ponderosas," page 31 and elsewhere, are a type of pine tree common to mountainous regions in western North America. The thick, resinous bark of mature ponderosas can be fire resistant; however, many cannot withstand the wildfires we have now.

"After the Deaths of Two Children," page 38, is for Mark Miller and Carma Miller.

"The Velocity of Sorrow," page 39, mentions the STEM School shooting in Highlands Ranch, Colorado, May 7, 2019. Nine students were shot; one died.

"Lamentation in Wind," page 41, is an elegy for Gordon Beesley—friend, neighbor, and police officer who was ambushed and killed in Arvada, Colorado, on June 21, 2021. The poem includes excerpts from Emily Dickinson's letter to Mrs. J.G. Holland, October 1879, accessed at http://archive.emilydickinson.org/correspondence/holland/l619.html.

"Hidden Narratives," pages 51-54: Sappho quotes in this poem are from *Sappho: A New Translation*, by Mary Barnard (University of California Press, Berkeley, 1958); and *Greek Lyric Poetry: A New Translation*, by Sherod Santos (W.W. Norton and Co., 2005).

"Lights Out," page 60, mentions *Gone*, a painting by Isabella Kirkland, accessed at https://www.isabellakirkland.com/gone.

About the Author

Radha Marcum is the author of *Bloodline* (3: A Taos Press, 2017), which received the 2018 New Mexico–Arizona Book Award in Poetry, and her poems appear frequently in journals including *Bennington Review*, *Gulf Coast*, *North American Review*, *Notre Dame Review*, *Pleiades*, and *Poetry Northwest*. Working as a prose writer with a focus on health and environment, she has written for organizations and media such as American Rivers, Colorado Water Trust, *Outside*, and The Wilderness Society. A graduate of Bennington College and the University of Washington, Seattle, where she held the Klepser Fellowship in Poetry, Marcum teaches at the Lighthouse Writers Workshop and privately. She lives in Colorado.

About The Word Works

Since its founding in 1974, The Word Works has steadily published volumes of contemporary poetry and presented public programs. Its imprints include The Washington Prize, The Tenth Gate Prize, The Hilary Tham Capital Collection, and International Editions.

Monthly, The Word Works offers free programs in its Café Muse Literary Salon. Starting in 2023, the winners of the Jacklyn Potter Young Poets Competition will be presented in the June Café Muse program.

As a 501(c)3 organization, The Word Works has received awards from the National Endowment for the Arts, the National Endowment for the Humanities, the D.C. Commission on the Arts & Humanities, the Witter Bynner Foundation, Poets & Writers, The Writer's Center, Bell Atlantic, the David G. Taft Foundation, and others, including many generous private patrons.

An archive of artistic and administrative materials in the Washington Writing Archive is housed in the George Washington University Gelman Library. The Word Works is a member of the Community of Literary Magazines and Presses and its books are distributed by Small Press Distribution.

wordworksbooks.org

WASHINGTON PRIZE WINNERS

Nathalie Anderson, *Following Fred Astaire*, 1998

Michael Atkinson, *One Hundred Children Waiting for a Train*, 2001

Molly Bashaw, *The Whole Field Still Moving Inside It*, 2013

Carrie Bennett, *biography of water*, 2004

Peter Blair, *Last Heat*, 1999

John Bradley, *Love-in-Idleness: The Poetry of Roberto Zingarello*, 1989, 2ND edition 2014

Christopher Bursk, *The Way Water Rubs Stone*, 1988

Richard Carr, *Ace*, 2008

Jamison Crabtree, *Rel[AM]ent*, 2014

Jessica Cuello, *Hunt*, 2016

Barbara Duffey, *Simple Machines*, 2015

B. K. Fischer, *St. Rage's Vault*, 2012

Linda Lee Harper, *Toward Desire*, 1995

Ann Rae Jonas, *A Diamond Is Hard But Not Tough*, 1997

Meg Kearney, *All Morning the Crows*, 2020

Annie Kim, *Eros, Unbroken*, 2019

Susan Lewis, *Zoom*, 2017

Frannie Lindsay, *Mayweed*, 2009

Richard Lyons, *Fleur Carnivore*, 2005

Elaine Magarrell, *Blameless Lives*, 1991

Fred Marchant, *Tipping Point*, 1993, 2ND edition 2013

Nils Michals, *Gembox*, 2018

Ron Mohring, *Survivable World*, 2003

Barbara Moore, *Farewell to the Body*, 1990

Naomi Mulvihill, *The Knife Thrower's Girl*, 2022

Brad Richard, *Motion Studies*, 2010

Jay Rogoff, *The Cutoff*, 1994

Prartho Sereno, *Call from Paris*, 2007, 2ND edition 2013

Enid Shomer, *Stalking the Florida Panther*, 1987

John Surowiecki, *The Hat City After Men Stopped Wearing Hats*, 2006

Sharon Suzuki-Martinez, *The Loneliest Whale Blues*, 2021

Miles Waggener, *Phoenix Suites*, 2002

Charlotte Warren, *Gandhi's Lap*, 2000

Mike White, *How to Make a Bird with Two Hands*, 2011

Nancy White, *Sun, Moon, Salt*, 1992, 2ND edition 2010

George Young, *Spinoza's Mouse*, 1996

www.ingramcontent.com/pod-product-compliance
Lightning Source LLC
Chambersburg PA
CBHW020332090426
42735CB00009B/1512